The Wildlife Trusts Guide to

INSECTS

The Wildlife Trusts Guide to

INSECTS

Series Editor Nicholas Hammond

Illustrated by
Sandra Doyle and Stuart Carter

NEW HOLLAND

First published in 2002 by
New Holland Publishers (UK) Ltd
London • Cape Town • Sydney • Auckland
www.newhollandpublishers.com

10 9 8 7 6 5 4 3 2

Garfield House, 86–88 Edgware Road, London W2 2EA, United Kingdom
80 McKenzie Street, Cape Town 8001, South Africa
14 Aquatic Drive, Frenchs Forest, NSW 2086, Australia
218 Lake Road, Northcote, Auckland, New Zealand

ISBN 1 85974 962 3

Publishing Manager: Jo Hemmings
Project Editor: Mike Unwin
Production: Joan Woodroffe

Packaged by Wildlife Art Ltd:
www.wildlife-art.co.uk
Design and Cover Design: Sarah Crouch
Art/Copy Editor: Sarah Whittley
Proof-reading and Index: Rachel Lockwood
Illustrators: Sandra Doyle, Stuart Carter

Reproduction by Modern Age
Repro Co. Ltd, Hong Kong
Printed and bound in Singapore by
Kyodo Printing Co (Singapore) Pte Ltd

Contents

Since 1912, The Wildlife Trusts have been speaking out for wildlife and undertaking practical action at the local level throughout the UK. Believing that wildlife is essential to a healthy environment for all, The Wildlife Trusts work with people from all walks of life – communities, industry, government, landowners, and families – to make sure nature gets a chance amongst all of the pressures of the modern world.

With years of experience and the service of the UK's top naturalists, The Wildlife Trusts and Wildlife Watch – the UK's leading club for young environmentalists – play a key part in restoring the balance between new developments and the natural world. With the specialist skills of volunteers and staff they manage more than 2,300 wildlife reserves (totalling more than 80,000 hectares), which are among the finest sites in the UK.

Their members, who number more than 366,000, contribute to their achievements by their generosity and hard work, and by spreading the message to everyone that wildlife matters.

The Wildlife Trusts is a registered charity (number 207238). For membership, and other details, please phone The Wildlife Trusts on 0870 0367711, or log on to www.wildlifetrusts.org

Insects are invertebrates, which means they have no internal skeleton. Instead they have an outer shell that contains the internal organs. They are distinguished from spiders and crustaceans by having six legs. During its lifetime an insect will go through a series of stages or metamorphoses. At each of these stages the insect changes its appearance quite dramatically. Already about a million species have been identified and more remain to be described. Almost 100,000 species of insect are found in Europe.

Insect structure

Some insects are so small that a microscope is needed to see them clearly, while some of the moths and dragonflies have wingspans of up to 12 cm. The form which they take is also very varied, but they do share certain anatomical characteristics. The bodies of adult insects have three main parts: the head, the thorax and the abdomen.

The head has a pair of compound eyes, whose surfaces are faceted with tiny lenses. The number of these lenses or facets varies, but dragonflies, which are swift fliers and active predators, have several thousand in each eye while some soil-dwelling insects may have none. In addition some insects have ocelli, very simple eyes on the front of the head, probably for detecting the intensity of light rather than producing images. There are two antennae, which are the sensors of smell and touch. Some species have simple antennae that are a series of similar segments well-supplied with nerve endings. In other species the antennae may be more complex: branched as in weevils or feather-shaped as in moths. The head also contains the mouth-parts which are complex and which vary according to the feeding methods of each species. The basis of the mouth-parts are a pair of jaws, a pair of secondary jaws and a lower lip. They also have four palps which examine the food before it is eaten. The secondary jaws and the lower lip hold the food steady while the other set of jaws cut it up.

The mouth-parts of species which feed on liquids have been modified quite dramatically. True bugs which feed on the sap of plants have piercing mouth-parts. Mosquitoes and horse-flies have long, needle-like jaws with which they pierce an animal's skin and withdraw its blood. Moths and butterflies have no jaws, but the secondary jaws have become linked together to form a long proboscis, through which they can suck nectar.

The thorax is the motor centre of the insect. It has three segments, on each of which are a pair of legs, The legs are variable, but have a femur or thigh, a tibia or shin, and a tarsus or foot. The second carries a pair of wings and, if there is a second pair of wings, they are on the third segment. Most insects have wings, but they are missing from the primitive bristletails and springtails and from the parasitic lice and fleas. The scientific name of many of the orders of insects describes their wings: Coleoptera (beetles) means "leather wings", Lepidoptera (moths and butterflies) means "scaly wings", Diptera (flies) means "two wings". The forewings of beetles are thick and leathery, providing a covering to the hindwings. In flight they are held upright.

The abdomen is the centre of digestion and excretion. It is also where the sexual organs are situated. Most insects have eleven abdomenal segments. At the tip there are a pair of cerci or tail-feelers. The male often has a pair of claspers on the ninth segment: these are used for holding the female while mating. Females have an ovipositor between the eighth and ninth segments, they are usually concealed inside the body. Some species, such as the ichneumons and the greater horntail, have long and exposed ovipositors. For bees and wasps, the ovipositor has lost its egg-laying function and has been replaced by a sting.

Life cycle of insects

It is well known that insects go through a series of developmental stages, or metamorphoses. However the nature and timing of these stages differ between groups and species. The first stage is the egg. The hatchling from the egg looks nothing like its parent, except in the case of some of the most primitive insects. The best known life-cycle is that of butterflies, whose larvae are caterpillars, which then pupate to become chrysalids, from which emerge the adult insects. The caterpillar's sole purpose is eating and as it grows it sheds its outer covering in a series of moults. As an insect moults it becomes slow and seeks cover because it is very vulnerable, which means the process of moulting is difficult to see in the wild. Dragonflies lay their eggs in water and the larvae develop underwater, emerging up the stems of plants and then shedding their larval casing to emerge as adult insects.

Grasshoppers have a partial metamorphosis with the young or nymphs looking like tiny adults and growing in a series of nymphal stages, shedding their skins several times until they reach adulthood.

The insects in this book appear within the orders to which they belong. These are listed below.

Odonata: Dragonflies and damselflies (page 10–18)
About 120 species of dragonfly and damselfly breed in Europe, 38 of which breed in the UK.

Orthoptera: Grasshoppers & crickets (page 19–21)

Dictyoptera: Cockroaches & mantids (page 22–23)
There are about 3,500 species worldwide. Three species are native to Britain. Of the world's 2,000 species of mantids, 18 are found in southern and central Europe.

Dermaptera: Earwigs (page 24)
Of the 1,300 known species, 34 occur in Europe and four in the British Isles.

Hemiptera: Bugs (page 25–33)
Roughly 75,000 species in this order of insects. In Europe there are 8,000 species, of which 1,700 are found in Britain and Ireland.

Neuroptera: Lacewings (page 34)
About 4,500 known species of which about 60 are British.

Mecoptera: Scorpion flies (page 35)
About 300 known species of which only four are found in the British Isles.

Trichoptera (page 36)
Almost 6,000 species worldwide with 189 in the United Kingdom.

Diptera: True flies (pages 37–51)
There are almost 100,000 known species worldwide and 5,200 occur in the British Isles.

Lepidoptera: Butterflies and moths
Over 100,000 species worldwide with 2,300 in Europe.

Hymenoptera: Ants, wasps, bees, sawflies & ichneumons (page 52–73)
Over 100,000 species in this order, with over 300 species in the British Isles.

Coleoptera: Beetles (pages 74–91)
Over 300,000 species of beetles. Europe has over 20,000 species and there are 4,000 species in Britain.

Blue-tailed damselfly
Ischnura elegans
SIZE AND DESCRIPTION 31 mm long, with a 30–40 mm wingspan. Dark bronze/black abdomen. Light-blue band on the 8th segment. Steady flier.
HABITAT Lowland pools and slow-flowing rivers. Usually the first damselfly to visit newly dug garden ponds. Absent from Iceland, Spain and most of Scandinavia.
FOOD/HABITS Flies early May to early September.

Common blue damselfly
Enallagama cyathigerum
SIZE AND DESCRIPTION 32 mm long, with a 36–42 mm wingspan. Male has a blue abdomen with black spots. The 8th and 9th segments are all blue. Female has a yellowish or bluish abdomen, with variable dark markings. Strong flier.
HABITAT Pools throughout Europe, except Iceland, Mediterranean islands, southern Italy and the Greek Peloponnese.
FOOD/HABITS Flies May to September.

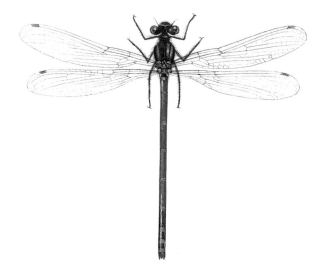

Large red damselfly
Pyrrhosoma nymphula
SIZE AND DESCRIPTION 36 mm long, with a 38–48 mm
wingspan. Red abdomen, with black markings from the
7th to 9th segments.
HABITAT Clear streams, ponds, lakes and canals across
Europe, except northern Scandinavia, Iceland and Sardinia.
FOOD/HABITS Flies late April to late September. Usually
in large numbers. Rests on marginal plants. Feeds on
small insects.

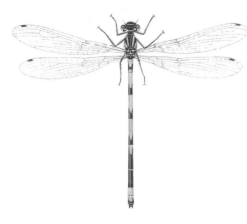

Azure damselfly
Coenagrion puella

SIZE AND DESCRIPTION 33 mm long, with a 36–44 mm wingspan. Male has a blue abdomen, with black markings and a completely blue 8th segment. Female has a dark abdomen, with blue or green markings.

HABITAT Pools and lakes up to 1,800 m. Found from Ireland and southern Scotland across Europe, and south to North Africa.

FOOD/HABITS Flies mid-May to late August. Often seen in sunny meadows.

Common hawker
Aeshna juncea

SIZE AND DESCRIPTION 74 mm long, with a wingspan of 95 mm. Male has a black abdomen, with pairs of blue spots and small yellow marks. Female is brown with yellow marks. Flies well and strongly.

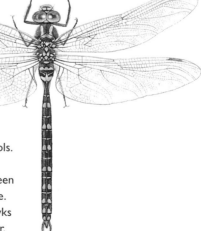

HABITAT Lakes, ponds, peat bogs and still pools. Found south from northern Norway to the Pyrenees. Absent from Iceland. Occurs between 800 m and 1,000 m in southern part of range.

FOOD/HABITS Flies late June to October. Hawks for other insects, often some way from water.

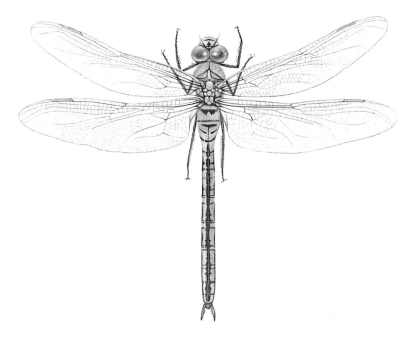

Emperor dragonfly
Anax imperator

SIZE AND DESCRIPTION A large dragonfly, 78 mm long, with a wingspan of 107 mm. The thorax is green, and the bright blue abdomen has a thick black stripe down the back. Females are usually green, but may be blue. Males fly strongly, patrolling territory above human head height.

HABITAT Pools, ponds, ditches and slow-flowing rivers across Europe, southwards from Denmark. Known to visit woodland rides and glades when hunting.

FOOD/HABITS Flies late May to mid-August. Hunts flies, moths and beetles, and will even take tadpoles from the water's surface.

Brown hawker
Aeshna grandis
SIZE AND DESCRIPTION 73 mm long, with a wingspan of 102 mm. Brown wings make this species unmistakable. Male has a brown abdomen with bright blue spots. Female has yellow markings on her brown abdomen. Both sexes have diagonal marks on the side of the thorax. Strong flier.
HABITAT Ponds, lakes, canals, peat bogs and slow-flowing rivers. Absent from Iceland, Iberia, Italy, Greece, Scotland and northern Scandinavia.
FOOD/HABITS Flies mid-June to mid-October. Hunts flies, mosquitoes, moths and butterflies.

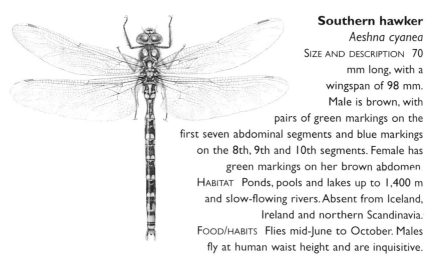

Southern hawker
Aeshna cyanea
SIZE AND DESCRIPTION 70 mm long, with a wingspan of 98 mm. Male is brown, with pairs of green markings on the first seven abdominal segments and blue markings on the 8th, 9th and 10th segments. Female has green markings on her brown abdomen. HABITAT Ponds, pools and lakes up to 1,400 m and slow-flowing rivers. Absent from Iceland, Ireland and northern Scandinavia. FOOD/HABITS Flies mid-June to October. Males fly at human waist height and are inquisitive.

Migrant hawker
Aeshna mixta
SIZE AND DESCRIPTION
63 mm long, wingspan of 87 mm. Male, dark brown and blue, has a bright blue spot on the side at the base of the abdomen. Brown female has small yellow spots. Neat, elegant, sometimes jerky flight. HABITAT Still or slow-flowing water. From England and Wales across Europe, south from the Baltic to North Africa. Adults migrate. FOOD/HABITS Flies July to October. Approachable.

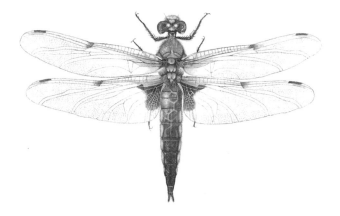

Four-spotted chaser
Libellula quadrimaculata
SIZE AND DESCRIPTION 43 mm long, wingspan of 76 mm. Broad
brown body, with yellow patches along each side. There are
two dark marks on the leading edge of each wing.
HABITAT Still water with plenty of vegetation. Found
throughout Europe, except Iceland.
FOOD/HABITS Flies mid-May to mid-August. Frequently
perches in the open and flies out over the water.
Aggressive and territorial nature.

Broad-bodied chaser
Libellula depressa
SIZE AND DESCRIPTION
44 mm long, wingspan of 76 mm. Male has flattened, fat, pale blue body, with yellow patches along each side. Brownish-yellow females have yellow spots along each side. Fast flier.
HABITAT Still or slow-flowing water, to 1,200 m. Across Europe from Wales and England, and from southern Sweden south to the Mediterranean.
FOOD/HABITS Flies early May to early August. Rests on waterside plants.

Ruddy darter
Sympetrum sanguineum
SIZE AND DESCRIPTION
34 mm long, wingspan of 55 mm. Males are blood-red, with the tip of the abdomen club-shaped, rather than tapering. Yellow females have black thorax markings. Flitting, sometimes jerky flight.
HABITAT Well-vegetated (even brackish or acid) pools up to 1,000 m. Found from Ireland across Europe, and south from southern Scandinavia.
FOOD/HABITS Flies June to October. Often perches.

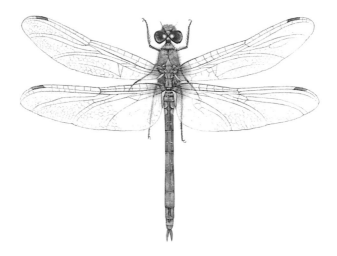

Common darter
Sympetrum striolatum

SIZE AND DESCRIPTION 37 mm long, wingspan of 57 mm. Males are red, with a narrow pointed abdomen. Females are greenish yellow. Flies busily.

HABITAT Ponds, lakes, ditches and brackish waters up to 1,800 m. Found across Europe from Ireland, and south from southern Scandinavia to North Africa.

FOOD/HABITS Flies June to October. Usually seen in large numbers. Often perches on twigs.

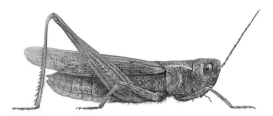

Common field grasshopper
Chorthippus brunneus
SIZE AND DESCRIPTION Body length: 14–18 mm (m); 19–25 mm (f). Colour green, purple or black. Wings are narrow, and extend beyond tip of the abdomen. Male's abdomen has a reddish tip, sometimes also occurs in the female. Song is a hard "sst" sound, repeated at 2-second intervals.
HABITAT Widespread in dry, grassy habitats, from Scandinavia to the Pyrenees and Italy. Particularly common in southern England.
FOOD/HABITS Adults are seen from July to October.

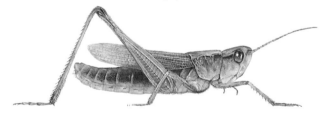

Meadow grasshopper
Chorthippus parallelus
SIZE AND DESCRIPTION Body length: 13–16 mm (m); 17–33 mm (f). Colour grey, green, brown or purple. Wings are short, reaching almost to the tip of the male's abdomen; female's even shorter, only half as long. Song is short, sewing-machine-like chirps in 1-second bursts.
HABITAT Northern Europe into Scandinavia, meadows and grassland. Absent from Ireland and Isle of Man. In the Mediterranean, it tends to occur in mountain regions.
FOOD/HABITS Adults are seen from June to November.

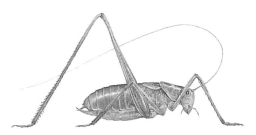

Speckled bushcricket
Leptophyes punctatissima
SIZE AND DESCRIPTION Body length: 10–14 mm (m); 12–17 mm (f). Yellow-green with fine red speckles. Male's abdomen has a narrow brown stripe along the top. Wings are short. Female has a long, sickle-shaped ovipositor. Song is a sequence of soft "zb" sounds at 3–6 second intervals.
HABITAT Gardens, parks and forest edges in undergrowth. Widespread from southern Scandinavia to the Mediterranean, including the British Isles.
FOOD/HABITS Adults are seen from July or August to October. The speckled bushcricket feeds on leaves, including those of raspberry and rose bushes.

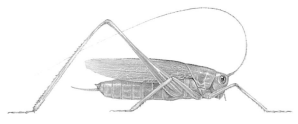

Oak bushcricket
Meconema thalassinum
SIZE AND DESCRIPTION Body length: 12–15 mm. Pale green, with wings extending beyond the tip of the abdomen. Female has a long, upward-curving ovipositor. Male has two thin, inward-curving cerci, about 3 mm long. Long yellow mark down the back, with two brown flecks on either side.
HABITAT Trees, particularly oaks. Southern Sweden to northern Spain, Italy.
FOOD/HABITS Adults are seen from July to October.

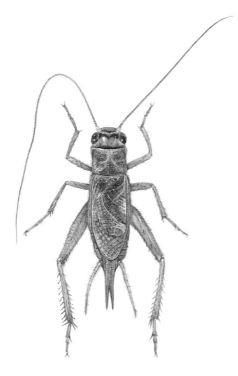

House cricket

Acheta domesticus

SIZE AND DESCRIPTION Body length: 16–20 cm. Straw-coloured to brown body, with black marks on the head. Wings extend beyond the tip of the abdomen. Female has a straight ovipositor, up to 15 mm long.

HABITAT The house cricket is a native insect of Asia and Africa, but is now widespread in Europe. It lives in buildings, but may also be found at refuse tips in summer. Song is a soft warble delivered at dusk or at night.

FOOD/HABITS Feeds on refuse, but will also eat stored food.

Common cockroach
Blatta orientalis
SIZE AND DESCRIPTION 18–30 mm long.
Male's leathery wings extend to the last
three segments of the abdomen; female's
wings barely cover the thorax.
HABITAT Warm indoor places, such as
kitchens. Rubbish tips in summer.
Survives outdoors in mild parts of
Europe. Originates from Asia and Africa.
FOOD/HABITS Scavenges on the ground
for food scraps and decaying matter.

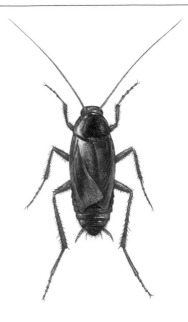

German cockroach
Blatta germanica
SIZE AND DESCRIPTION 10–13 mm long.
Pale reddish-brown. The long wings
extend beyond the tip of the abdomen.
There are two dark, longitudinal marks
on the pronotum (the shield covering
the head). Can fly, but rarely does so.
HABITAT Buildings, refuse-tips in
summer. Introduced from North Africa.
FOOD/HABITS Scavenges for food on
the ground.

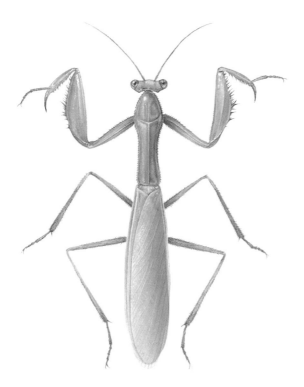

Praying mantis
Mantis religiosa

SIZE AND DESCRIPTION 20 mm long. Green body, sometimes brown. Males are particularly slender.

HABITAT Rough grassland, scrub and maquis in Europe, as far south as southern France.

FOOD/HABITS Preys on other insects. Adopts a threat display, raising the neck and front legs in a "praying" posture. Female eats the male after or during copulation.

Common earwig
Forficula auricularia
SIZE AND DESCRIPTION Body length:
10–15 mm; pincers measure 4–9 mm in
the male and 4–5 mm in the female.
HABITAT Abundant throughout Europe,
in a wide range of habitats. Very
common in gardens.
FOOD/HABITS Mainly vegetarian. White
earwigs found in the garden are in the
process of moulting. Displays parental
care for its young when disturbed.

Small earwig
Labia minor
SIZE AND DESCRIPTION Body length: 5
mm; pincers up to 2.5 mm long. Dull,
darkish-brown body and a blackish
head. Hindwings extend beyond
forewings when at rest.
HABITAT Found anywhere there is
decaying vegetation. Common around
compost heaps.
FOOD/HABITS Flies well, mostly at dusk.
Breeds in manure heaps. Displays
parental care for young.

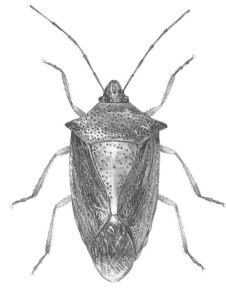

Hawthorn shield bug
Acanthosoma haemorrhoidale
SIZE AND DESCRIPTION   15 mm long.
Body is shield-shaped, with a
reddish-brown band along the rear
of the thorax.
HABITAT   Woodland edges, hedgerows
and gardens with hedges and shrubs.
Widespread in Europe, but absent
from Scotland.
FOOD/HABITS   Eats leaves of hawthorn
and fruit trees. Basks on walls in
autumn before hibernating.

Forest bug
Pentatoma rufipes
SIZE AND DESCRIPTION   12–15 mm long.
Dark brown, with a thorax that
protrudes like a yoke. Reddish legs.
HABITAT   Found on trees (particularly
cherry trees) in orchards
and shrubberies.
FOOD/HABITS   Adults are seen between
June and October. An omnivorous bug
that sucks juice from buds, leaves and
fruits, and attacks other insects.

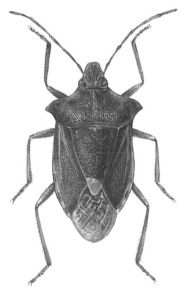

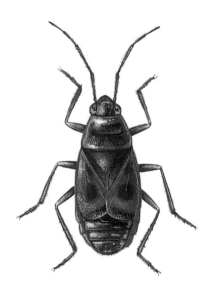

Fire bug
Pyrrhocoris apterus
SIZE AND DESCRIPTION 10 mm long. Red and black, with black spots on the red forewings.
HABITAT Found in open country in central and southern Europe.
FOOD/HABITS The fire bug is omnivorous, feeding on fallen seeds and preying upon other insects. Adults hibernate.

Green shield bug
Palomena prasina
SIZE AND DESCRIPTION 10–15 mm long. Bright green in spring and summer, bronze-coloured in autumn. Wing tips are dark brown.
HABITAT Woodland edges and glades, hedgerows and gardens with shrubs and herbaceous borders over much of Europe.
FOOD/HABITS Eats leaves of trees, shrubs and herbaceous plants. Hibernates in leaf litter.

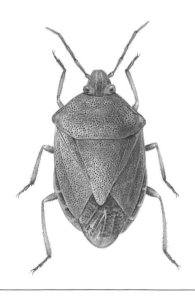

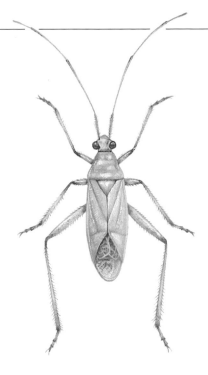

Black-kneed capsid
Blepharidopterus angulatus
SIZE AND DESCRIPTION 15 mm long.
Green, with a narrower body than that
of the common green capsid. Legs have
black patches on the "knees".
HABITAT Orchard trees, particularly
apples and limes.
FOOD/HABITS This predatory insect is
beneficial to orchard owners, as it
feeds on red spider mites, which cause
damage to fruit trees. Makes a "squeak"
by rubbing the tip of its beak against its
thorax. Will stab people with its beak
if handled.

Common flower bug
Anthocoris nemorum
SIZE AND DESCRIPTION 3–4 mm. Shiny
and generally brownish, with a black
spot on the greyish forewings. Head
is black.
HABITAT Found on almost any type of
tree, shrub or herbaceous plant.
Occurs over most of Europe.
FOOD/HABITS A predator of aphids, red
spider mites and other insects. Adults
hibernate under loose bark and in
clumps of grass.

Common green capsid
Lygocoris pabulinus
SIZE AND DESCRIPTION 5–7 mm long.
Green, with greyish wing-tips. Bristly
legs. The potato capsid is similar, but
has two black spots behind its head.
HABITAT Across most of Europe,
wherever there is plentiful vegetation.
FOOD/HABITS Flies from May to
October. Eggs laid on woody plants
hatch in spring. Eats herbaceous plants,
potatoes and soft fruits such as
raspberries and gooseberries.

Water measurer
Hydrometra stagnorum
SIZE AND DESCRIPTION 11 mm long, with
a narrow body, greatly elongated head
and long legs. Usually without wings.
HABITAT Found on the surface of still
or slow-flowing water across much
of Europe.
FOOD/HABITS Feeds on water fleas,
insect larvae and other small animals,
which it spears from the surface with
its beak. Moves slowly across
the surface.

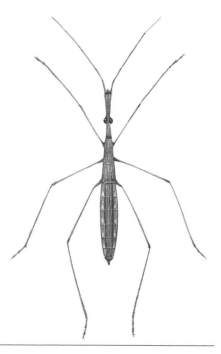

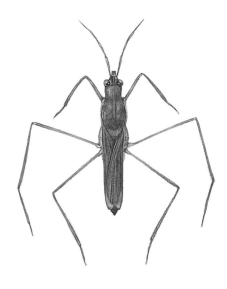

Common pond skater
Gerris lacustris
SIZE AND DESCRIPTION 10 mm long. Has a broader body than the water measurer and a considerably shorter head, which has largish eyes. Usually fully-winged. Several similar species.
HABITAT Lives on the surface of slow-moving water.
FOOD/HABITS Flies away from water to hibernate. When swimming, it moves across the water's surface with a rowing action of the middle legs. Hindlegs act as rudders, while front legs catch insects that fall into the water.

Water scorpion
Nepa cinerea
SIZE AND DESCRIPTION Body is 20 mm long, with a tail measuring 8 mm. The brown, flattened body is equipped with strong front legs. Fully-winged, but rarely flies.
HABITAT Lives in shallow water and at pond margins.
FOOD/HABITS Breathes through the hollow, snorkel-like "tail", which draws in air as it protrudes above the surface. Active throughout the year, the water scorpion feeds on invertebrates and small fish, which are caught with the powerful front legs.

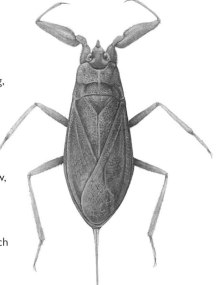

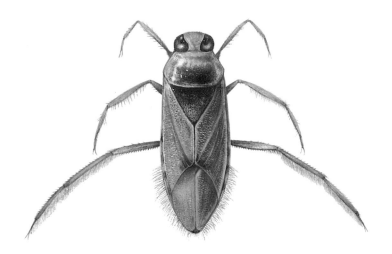

Common backswimmer
Notonecta glauca

SIZE AND DESCRIPTION 16 mm long. Has long, bristly hindlegs.
Swims on its back, which is keeled, clutching a large
air-bubble to its underside. There are several species of
water boatman.

HABITAT Swims in still water, and will fly in warm weather.

FOOD/HABITS A hunter of tadpoles, small fish and other
insects. Active all year round.

Cicada
Cicadetta montana

SIZE AND DESCRIPTION 18 mm long. Long transparent and shiny wings. Dark pronotum. Three spines on front femur.
HABITAT Woodland clearings and scrubby areas in central and southern Europe. Only in New Forest in Britain.
FOOD/HABITS Flies from May to August. Feeds on shrubs and herbaceous plants. Male produces soft warble by vibrating small membranes on abdomen.

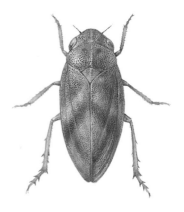

Common froghopper
Philaenus spumarius
SIZE AND DESCRIPTION 6 mm long.
Variable brown pattern. Wings held
together like a tent. Young coat
themselves in a white broth called
"cuckoo-spit".
HABITAT Woody and herbaceous plants
across Europe, except in the far north.
FOOD/HABITS Flies from June to
September. Feeds on plant sap.

Rose aphid
Macrosiphum rosae
SIZE AND DESCRIPTION 1–2 mm long.
Green or pink greenfly. Long
black cornicles on abdomen not found
on other aphids.
HABITAT Woodland edges, hedges and
gardens across Europe.
FOOD/HABITS Feeds on roses in spring
and scabious or teasel in summer.

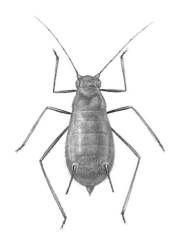

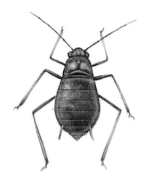

Black bean aphid
Aphis fabae
SIZE AND DESCRIPTION 2 mm. Black or olive in colour. May be wingless.
HABITAT All over Europe where there are suitable food plants.
FOOD/HABITS Feeds on young shoots of dock, beans, spinach, beet, nasturtium and other plants. Eggs are laid on shrubs such as spindle and philadelphius.

Woolly aphid
Eriosoma langerum
SIZE AND DESCRIPTION 1–2 mm long. Purplish-brown, with or without wings, and covered with strands of whitish, fluffy wax.
HABITAT Orchards and gardens across Europe. Accidentally introduced from America.
FOOD/HABITS Sucks the sap of fruit trees. Most young are born live by parthogenesis.

Green lacewing
Chrysopa pallens

SIZE AND DESCRIPTION 15–20 mm long; wingspan of 30–40 mm. Bright green body, golden eyes and green veins on transparent wings. Several continental species; two similar species in British Isles.

HABITAT Woods, hedgerows, gardens and well-vegetated areas. Most of Europe, but not Scotland and northern Scandinavia.

FOOD/HABITS Mainly nocturnal. Adults and young prey on aphids. Flies May to August.

Scorpion fly

Panorpa communis

SIZE AND DESCRIPTION 15 mm long; wingspan of 30 mm. Head has a "beak". Scorpion-like tip to male's abdomen. Several similar species.

HABITAT Woods, hedgerows and shaded gardens throughout Europe, except in the far north.

FOOD/HABITS Flies (weakly) from May to August. Eats mainly animal material. Larvae scavenge in soil.

Caddis fly
Phryganea grandis

SIZE AND DESCRIPTION The largest caddis fly in the UK with a wingspan of 64 mm. Resembles a small moth, with short hairs on wings. Long antennae, almost the length of wings. Broad dusty-brown wings. Male is smaller and lacks black stripe in forewing.

HABITAT Slow moving rivers and streams across most of Europe except far south.

FOOD/HABITS Larvae makes a protective case out of pieces of leaf, up to 50 mm long. It lives in this, dragging it around like a snail's shell. Feeds on plants and other insect larvae. Adults live for about one week. Fly mostly at night and are attracted to light.

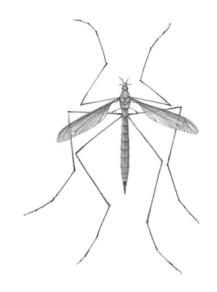

Common crane-fly or daddy-long-legs
Tipula paludosa

SIZE AND DESCRIPTION About 25 mm long. Dark brown along the leading edges of the wings. The female's wings are shorter than its abdomen. The male has a square-ended abdomen, while the female's is pointed with an ovipositor. Dull brown grub is known as a "leather-jacket".

HABITAT Common in grasslands, parks and gardens throughout Europe.

FOOD/HABITS Flies throughout the year, but most numerous in autumn. Adults rarely feed. Grubs live in the soil and appear at night to gnaw the base of plant stems.

Spotted crane-fly
Nephrotoma appendiculata

SIZE AND DESCRIPTION 15–25 mm long, with a largely yellow abdomen, often with black spots. The female is larger than the male and has a pointed tip to the abdomen, while the male's abdomen is clubbed. Wings are clear and shiny. Fat, dark brown "leather-jacket" grub.

HABITAT Common in farmland, parks and gardens across Europe.

FOOD/HABITS Flies May to August. Adults rarely feed, but the grubs feed on roots and do considerable damage to garden plants.

Gall midge
Jaapiella veronicae
SIZE AND DESCRIPTION 2 mm long.
Pointed tip to abdomen, which is pale
yellow. Wings are hairy. Fine, bead-like
antennae. Larvae are tiny and orange.
HABITAT Open areas with small plants.
FOOD/HABITS Flies in swarms on
summer evenings, often entering
lighted windows. Grubs live inside
germander speedwell plants and create
hairy galls on the tips of shoots.

Chironomid midge
Chironomus plumosus
SIZE AND DESCRIPTION About 8 mm
long. Wings are shorter than the
abdomen and held over the body at
rest. Male's antennae are very bushy.
Reddish aquatic larva is known as a
"bloodworm".
HABITAT Must have a body of water in
which to lay eggs. This may be relatively
small, such as a water butt.
FOOD/HABITS Adults rest on walls
as they dry out after emerging from
pupae. Non-biting.

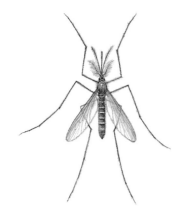

Common gnat
Culex pipiens
SIZE AND DESCRIPTION About 6 mm
long. Wings extend beyond abdomen's
tip. Female has a rounded tip to its
abdomen. Male has hairy antennae.
Holds the abdomen parallel to the
surface on which it is perching. Aquatic
larvae live beneath the surface.
HABITAT Abundant throughout Europe.
FOOD/HABITS Flies at night with
monotonous hum. Rarely bites humans,
preferring birds. Eggs are laid in rafts
on surface. Larvae dangle beneath
surface. Pupae swim to the bottom
to escape danger. Adults hibernate
in sheds.

Mosquito
Theobaldia annulata
SIZE AND DESCRIPTION About 6 mm long
this is the largest mosquito. Has white
rings around the legs. Dark spots on
the wings are formed by convergences
of veins.
HABITAT Widespread where there is
stagnant water for breeding.
FOOD/HABITS Adult females are blood-
sucking and require blood before they
can lay fertile eggs. Males feed on
nectar and other plant juices. Females
hibernate in sheds.

St. Mark's fly
Bibio marci
SIZE AND DESCRIPTION 10–12 mm long. Black, heavy-looking
fly whose dangling, hairy legs add to the impression of a
lumbering flight. Larva is primitive, with a large head.
HABITAT Gardens, woodland edges and well-vegetated open
country across Europe.
FOOD/HABITS Flies in late April and May (St. Mark's day is
25 April). Suns itself on walls and flowers. Larvae live
beneath the soil, eating rotting material.

Fever-fly
Dilophus febrilis
SIZE AND DESCRIPTION About 4 mm long. Black, but not hairy (compare St. Mark's fly). Female has smoky, almost opaque wings, while male's are almost clear with a black mark.
HABITAT Abundant in most open habitats.
FOOD/HABITS Flies from March to October, but is commonest in spring. Large flocks may cluster on grass stems. Males often hover sluggishly. Larvae live beneath the soil in decaying matter, but may damage roots.

Cleg-fly
Haematopota pluvialis
SIZE AND DESCRIPTION About 10 mm long. Dull grey, with a rather cylindrical abdomen. The wings are mottled. Holds its wings above the abdomen when at rest. Flies silently
HABITAT Common from May to September, especially in damp woods. Replaced in north and upland areas by another similar species.
FOOD/HABITS Flies May to October. Often seen in thundery weather. Females are bloodsuckers, biting human beings and livestock. Males drink nectar and plant juices. The larvae live in the soil, where they prey on other invertebrates.

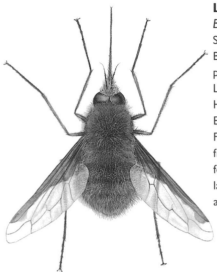

Large bee-fly
Bombylius major
SIZE AND DESCRIPTION 10–12 mm.
Brown, furry, bee-like coat and a long
proboscis. Dark leading edge to wings.
Legs are long and slender.
HABITAT Wooded places across
Europe, but rare in far north.
FOOD/HABITS Hovers, using its long
front legs to steady itself as it reaches
for nectar with its long proboscis. The
larvae are parasitic on solitary bees
and wasps.

Window-fly
Scenopinus fenestratus
SIZE AND DESCRIPTION About 7 mm long.
Small, black and without bristles. Reddish-
brown legs, sometimes with black markings.
Wings are tightly folded when at rest.
HABITAT Often seen at windows,
particularly in old buildings.
FOOD/HABITS Seems reluctant to fly,
apparently preferring to walk away
when disturbed. Larvae live in birds'
nests and buildings, preying on other
insects and their larvae.

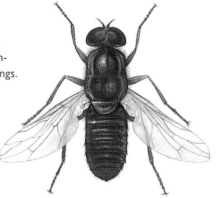

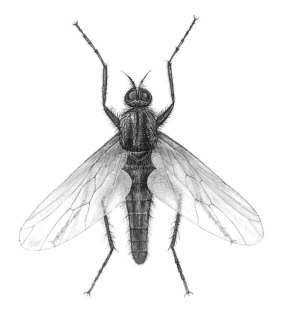

Dance-fly
Empis tessellata

SIZE AND DESCRIPTION 10–12 mm long. Dark grey, with a small head, pointed proboscis and sturdy thorax. Long hairy legs.
HABITAT Woodland edges, hedges, gardens and open habitats with shrubs.
FOOD/HABITS Flies April to August. Hops among hawthorn or umbellifer flowers. Probes blossom and hunts for other insects, which it pierces with its proboscis. May be seen on the wing carrying flies it has caught.

Hover-fly
Scaeva pyrastri
SIZE AND DESCRIPTION   12–15 mm long.
Black abdomen with six bold cream
crescents. Rounded abdomen.
Slug-like larva.
HABITAT   Flower-rich habitats across
much of Europe, but not northern
Scandinavia and rare in Scotland.
FOOD/HABITS   Adults seen flying from
May to November, but most commonly
seen in late summer. Feeds on nectar
and honeydew. Larvae feed on aphids.

Hover-fly
Syrphus ribesii
SIZE AND DESCRIPTION   About 10 mm long.
Yellow and black striped with rounded
abdomen. Larva is green and slug-like.
There are several similar species.
HABITAT   Flower-rich habitats across
Europe.
FOOD/HABITS   Flying adults seen from
March to November. Males perch on
leaves or twigs up to 2.5 metres from
the ground and make high-pitched
whining song. Feeds mainly on nectar,
but will crush and swallow pollen.
Larvae feed on aphids.

Hover-fly
Volucella zonaria

SIZE AND DESCRIPTION 15–25 mm long. Abdomen with
chestnut at front with two yellow-orange and black stripes
and brown tinge to wings near the thorax gives hornet-like
appearance.

HABITAT Woodlands, woodland edges and gardens from
Mediterranean to southern England.

FOOD/HABITS Flies between May and November. Feeds on
nectar, pollen and honeydew. Larvae scavenge in wasps' nests.

Hover-fly
Melanostroma scalare
SIZE AND DESCRIPTION 6–9 mm long.
Narrow abdomen with yellow marks.
Male's abdomen narrower than
female's. Female's abdomen narrows
towards thorax.
HABITAT Common in herb-rich areas
and gardens.
FOOD/HABITS Flies between April and
November. Often seen on hawthorn
blossom in May. Larvae feed on aphids.

Drone-fly
Eristalis tenax
SIZE AND DESCRIPTION 10–15 mm long.
Looks like a honey bee drone. Dark
anvil marks on abdomen. Larva is called
a "rat-tailed maggot" because of its
long rear breathing tube.
HABITAT Very common in parks,
gardens and other flower-rich places
across Europe.
FOOD/HABITS Nectar and pollen eater.
Can be seen throughout the year. Larva
lives in stagnant water, sewage, and
dung-hills.

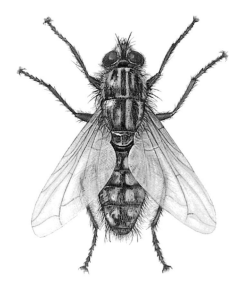

Flesh-fly
Sarcophaga carnaria

SIZE AND DESCRIPTION 12–20 mm. Red eyes. Grey and black chequered abdomen. Large feet.

HABITAT Often seen around houses, but rarely indoors. Wide range of habitats throughout Europe.

FOOD/HABITS Active throughout the year. Feeds as adult on nectar, rotting carrion and dung. Females are live-bearers. Maggots feed in dung and carrion.

Narcissus-fly
Merodon equestris
SIZE AND DESCRIPTION   10–15 mm long.
Bumble bee mimic with black legs, with
prominent bulge on hind-legs and hairy
brownish yellow abdomen.
HABITAT   Gardens, parks, woods and
hedges across Europe except the
far north.
FOOD/HABITS   Commonest in May but
flies from March to August. Eggs are
laid in the base of daffodils and other
bulbs. Larvae burrow down into bulbs.

Fruit-fly
Drosophilia funebris
SIZE AND DESCRIPTION   About 3 mm
long. Small dark brown fly. One of many
similar species.
HABITAT   Widespread in gardens, farms,
orchards and food factories.
FOOD/HABITS   Attracted by rotting fruit,
vinegar, wine and other fermenting
material. Commonest in summer and
autumn, but present all year in food
and drink factories. Larvae feed on
decaying vegetable matter.

Bluebottle

Calliphora vomitoria

SIZE AND DESCRIPTION 12–15 mm long. Rounded metallic blue body. Creamy white, carrot-shaped larva.

HABITAT Widespread throughout Europe. Often seen in and around houses.

FOOD/HABITS Seen all year round, often sunning themselves on walls. Eggs are laid on meat and carrion, on which larvae feed.

Diptera

Common house-fly
Musca domestica
SIZE AND DESCRIPTION 8 mm long.
Black and tan abdomen.
HABITAT In and around houses
throughout Europe. Especially
numerous in places where there is
plenty of decaying matter.
FOOD/HABITS Found most of the
year, but most common from June
to September.

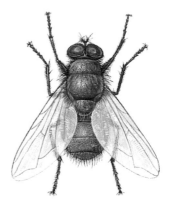

Greenbottle
Lucilia caesar
SIZE AND DESCRIPTION 8–15 mm long.
Abdomen varies from blue-green to
emerald and becoming coppery with
age. Silvery below the eyes.
HABITAT Most habitats across Europe.
Common around houses but rarely
seen indoors.
FOOD/HABITS Adults feed on nectar and
carrion juices. Larvae feed on carrion
and may be found in wounds on animals.

Cabbage root-fly
Delia radicum
SIZE AND DESCRIPTION 5–7 mm long.
Bristly black or dark grey abdomen.
HABITAT All over Europe wherever
there are crucifers growing.
FOOD/HABITS Flies March to November
and feeds on nectar. Larvae feed on
roots of brassicae and oilseed rape,
causing leaves to become limp
and yellow.

Yellow dung-fly
Scathophaga stercoraria
SIZE AND DESCRIPTION 8 mm long. Males
are covered with golden yellow fur.
Females are grayish and less furry.
HABITAT Places where there is dung
from horses and cows across Europe.
FOOD/HABITS Adults fly for much of the
year, preying on other flies on cow-
dung. Adults develop in cow-pats.

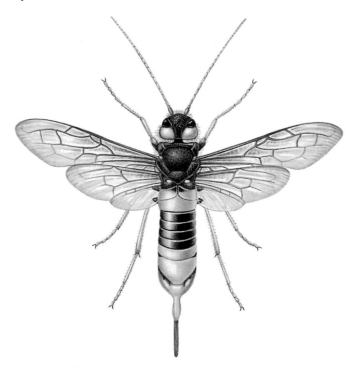

Horntail

Urceros gigas

SIZE AND DESCRIPTION Up to 40 mm long, including the ovipositor. Female is black and yellow. The male is smaller with an orange abdomen with a black tip and orange legs.
HABITAT Coniferous woodland, but can survive in treated timber, from which they may appear in new houses.
FOOD/HABITS Despite the fearsome appearance of the females, horntails are harmless. Fly in sunshine from May to October. Males usually fly near tree tops. Females drill into bark and deposit eggs in the trunk. Larvae are almost legless and feed on the timber.

Hawthorn sawfly
Trichiosoma tibiale
SIZE AND DESCRIPTION
20 mm long. Leathery
wings with hairy abdomen
and thorax. Larva is pale green
with brown head.
HABITAT Hedgerows, scrubby places
and other habitats with hawthorn in
northern and central Europe.
FOOD/HABITS Flies in May and June.
Larva feeds on hawthorn and spins a
tough cocoon in which it pupates and
from which the adult bites its way out.

Yellow ophion
Ophion luteus
SIZE AND DESCRIPTION 15–20 mm.
Yellowish brown, strongly arched
abdomen and thorax. Large black eyes.
HABITAT Well-vegetated habitats throughout
most Europe except the far north.
FOOD/HABITS Adults fly from July to
October. Attracted by light. Feeds on nectar and
pollen. Eggs are laid in caterpillars or pupae of
several species. There is usually one grub per host.
The adult always emerges from the host's pupa.

Gooseberry sawfly

Nematus ribesii

SIZE AND DESCRIPTION Up to 10 mm.
Female has yellow abdomen. Male has
black abdomen and is thinner. Green
larva with black head.

HABITAT Common in gardens over
most of Europe, except the far north.

FOOD/HABITS Adults fly from April to
September. Larvae feed gregariously
on leaves of gooseberry and currants.
Pupates in the soil.

Ichneumon fly

Apanteles glomeratus

SIZE AND DESCRIPTION 3–4 mm long.
Black with smoky wings and brown
legs. Larvae are pale brown, small and
almost translucent.

HABITAT Found throughout Europe in
cultivated areas and places where its
host is found.

FOOD/HABITS Adults fly in two broods
in summer. Eggs are laid in caterpillars
of large white and black-veined white.
Up to 150 grubs emerge inside the
caterpillar and devour it to leave an
empty skin.

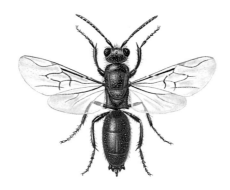

Rubytail wasp

Chrysis ignita

SIZE AND DESCRIPTION 7–10 mm long. Abdomen is brilliant red or purple. Head is blue-green with a golden sheen.

HABITAT A wide range of open habitats throughout Europe.

FOOD/HABITS Adults fly from April to September, feeding on nectar. May be seen on walls and tree trunks searching for nests of mason wasps in which to lay eggs. Larvae feed on grubs of host and food stored by host.

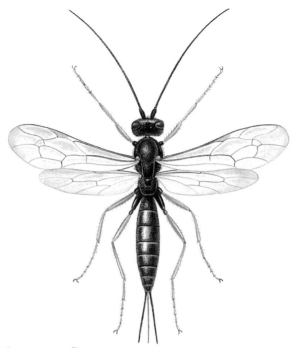

Ichnuemon fly
Pimpla instigator

SIZE AND DESCRIPTION 10–24 mm. This is the commonest of all the 4,000 ichnuemon fly species found across Europe. The body is black with obvious orange legs. The female has an ovipositor, which is roughly half the length of her abdomen.

HABITAT Most habitats throughout Europe. Present all summer.

FOOD/HABITS An ectoparasite of moth larvae, especially the snout moth. The female can inject as many as 150 eggs into a defenseless caterpillar. The grubs grow inside the caterpillar, feeding on its body.

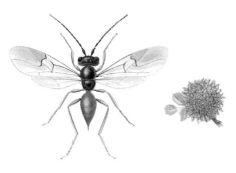

Robin's pincushion
Diplolepis rosae
SIZE AND DESCRIPTION About 4 mm
long. Black head and thorax. Orange
abdomen and legs. Reddish orange gall
on wild roses. Whitish grub.
HABITAT Open countryside, woodland
edges, gardens and parks with
wild roses.
FOOD/HABITS Flies from April to June.
Males are very rare and females lay
eggs without mating. Galls mature
in autumn.

Spangle/Currant gall wasp
Neuroterus quercusbaccarum
SIZE AND DESCRIPTION 2.75 mm long.
Black with brown legs and antennae.
Galls are brownish circles on underside
of oak leaves, giving the impression of
spangling or small and spherical like currants.
HABITAT Oak trees.
FOOD/HABITS Galls appear on leaves in late summer.
In autumn the gall and its grub drop to the ground.
The larvae pupates during the winter. The adults that
emerge in February and March are all females which
lay eggs on leaves and oak buds without fertilization.

Oak apple gall wasp
Biorhiza pallida
SIZE AND DESCRIPTION 1.7 to 2.8 mm. Small, brown wasp. Galls are spherical, reaching more than 30 mm in diameter.
HABITAT Oak trees.
FOOD/HABITS Oak apples appear on oaks in April or May. Males and females emerge from the galls in June or July. Males appear a day or two in advance of the females and the galls often contain only one sex. Females deposit eggs in the roots of the oak. Each gall is only about 10 mm in diameter and contains a single larva. The adults, which emerge in December or January, are all wingless females. These crawl up the tree to lay eggs in buds in the canopy. These result in oak apple galls and the sexual generation of gall wasps.

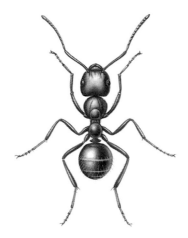

Black garden ant

Lasius niger

SIZE AND DESCRIPTION Workers are up to 5 mm long. They are black or dark brown, and the pedicel is a single segment. Flying ants, which emerge in July and August, are males and females. They are about twice the size of workers. Black garden ants do not sting.

HABITAT Open habitats throughout Europe, including gardens.

FOOD/HABITS Omnivorous, but is especially fond of sweet foods and will "milk" aphids for their honeydew. A colony consists of one queen and several thousand workers. Winged males and females emerge for mating flights in summer. Males die after mating; females break off their wings and seek a suitable nesting site. Birds take a heavy toll of the ants during mating flights. Very few females survive to create new colonies.

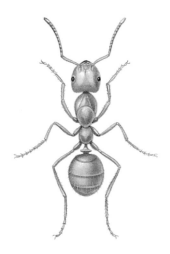

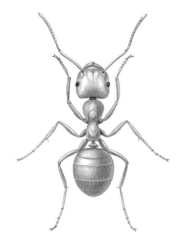

Yellow meadow ant
Lasius flavus

SIZE AND DESCRIPTION Workers are up to 4 mm long. They are yellowish-brown, with a single-segmented pedicel. Males and females fly in July and August and are about twice the size of workers. The queen is darker. Yellow meadow ants do not sting.

HABITAT Orchards and rough grassland across Europe.

FOOD/HABITS Creates the anthills that are a characteristic feature of rough grassland. Mating flocks can be very numerous.

Yellow lawn ant
Lasius umbratus

SIZE AND DESCRIPTION Workers are 4–5 mm long and yellowish.

HABITAT Grassy places across Europe.

FOOD/HABITS Lives almost entirely below ground; usually only seen when the lawn is dug up.

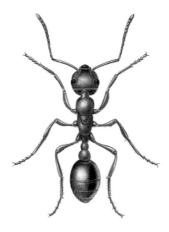

Red ant
Myrmica rubra

SIZE AND DESCRIPTION Workers are 4–5 mm long. They are chestnut brown, with a pedicel of two segments. Males and queens, which appear in late summer and early autumn, are about one-and-a-half times as long as workers. Males have longer, less bulbous abdomens than females. Red ants can sting.

HABITAT Open habitats throughout Europe.

FOOD/HABITS Omnivorous, and, although less inclined towards honeydew than the black ant, it tends towards animal food. A colony contains one or more queens and a few hundred workers.

Mason wasp
Ancistrocerus parietinus
SIZE AND DESCRIPTION 10–14 mm long.
Black and yellow, with a squarish black
mark on the first yellow band of its
pear-shaped abdomen.
HABITAT Common almost anywhere
in Europe.
FOOD/HABITS Adults fly April to August.
Feeds mainly on nectar and honeydew.
The female makes a mud nest in a
mortar cavity or natural crevice,
and then stocks the nest with
paralysed caterpillars.

German wasp
Vespula germanica
SIZE AND DECRIPTION
Workers 12–16 mm. Looks
very like the common wasp,
but has marks on either side
of the thorax bulge.
HABITAT Common in most habitats,
except in northern Scandinavia.
FOOD/HABITS Nesting habits are similar
to those of the common wasp, but the
nest-paper is greyer and less brittle.

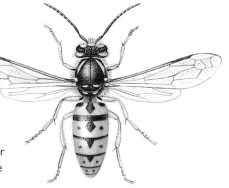

Common wasp
Vespula vulgaris

SIZE AND DECRIPTION Workers are 11–14 mm long. Black and yellow. Look for four yellow spots at the rear of the thorax. The yellow marks on either side of thorax usually have parallel sides.

HABITAT Common in most habitats across Europe.

FOOD/HABITS Usually nests in well-drained underground sites, such as hedgebanks, but will also use cavities in walls and lofts. Nests are built of yellowish paper.

Hornet
Vespa crabro
SIZE AND DECRIPTION Workers 18–25 mm. Chestnut brown
and yellow.
HABITAT Wooded areas, parks and gardens over most of
Europe, except Scotland, Ireland and northern Scandinavia.
FOOD/HABITS Nests in hollow trees, wall cavities and
chimneys. Preys on insects as large as butterflies and
dragonflies, to feed young.

Mining bee
Andrena haemorrhoa
SIZE AND DESCRIPTION   10–12 mm long.
Dark abdomen has a yellow tip, which
is larger in the male. Female has a
white face, while the male's face is
pale brown.
HABITAT Woodland edges, scrub
and gardens in northern and
central Europe.
FOOD/HABITS An early spring species,
which seeks nectar from blackthorn,
sallow and dandelions. Solitary species.

Flower bee
Anthophora plumipes
SIZE AND DESCRIPTION   14–16 mm long.
Female is black, with hairy
yellow-orange legs. Male has a
rusty-brown thorax and a darkish
tip to the abdomen. Looks like a
bumble bee, but has a large eye that
reaches the jaw.
HABITAT Many well-drained habitats.
Common around human settlements.
Much of Europe, but not Scotland.
FOOD/HABITS Flies from March to June.
Feeds on nectar, using its long tongue
to reach into tubular flowers. Nests
in soil and soft mortar.

Tawny mining bee
Andrena fulva

SIZE AND DESCRIPTION 10–12 mm long. Female has a bright yellow abdomen, while the male, which is smaller, is dark.
HABITAT Open habits, including gardens, parks and woodland edges. Central and southern Europe, including southern England.
FOOD/HABITS Flies April to June. Nests in the ground, especially on lawns, throwing spoil from the nest hole into a small, volcano-like mound. Solitary species.

Wool carder bee
Anthidium manicatum

SIZE AND DESCRIPTION 11 mm long. Thorax is black. Abdomen is black with yellow marks on either side. Legs are yellow. Not very hairy. Males are notably larger than females.
HABITAT Anywhere with flowers. Widespread across Europe.
FOOD/HABITS Flies June to August. Collects hairs from plants, which it carries in a ball beneath its body to take back to nest-holes in timber and masonry.

Mason bee
Osmia rufa

SIZE AND DESCRIPTION 8–13 mm long. Black head and thorax, with reddish-brown hair on the abdomen. The female is larger than the male, but the male has longer antennae. There are curved, bull-like horns between the female's antennae.
HABITAT Anywhere with flowers and suitable nest-holes across central and southern Europe, including southern England.
FOOD/HABITS Flies April to July. Nests are in holes, and composed of several cells of mud.

White-tailed bumble bee
Bombus lucorum
SIZE AND DESCRIPTION 20–22 mm long.
Yellow collar and second abdominal
segment, with white tip
to abdomen.
HABITAT Well-vegetated
places throughout Europe.
FOOD/HABITS A very early
flier, with queens emerging in
February and feeding on sallow
catkins. Nests below ground.

Buff-tailed bumble bee
Bombus terrestris
SIZE AND DESCRIPTION 20–22 mm long.
Orange collar and
second abdominal
segment. The tip of the
abdomen is buffish-white;
queen's abdominal tip is buffish
in British Isles, but white elsewhere.
HABITAT Well-vegetated habitats
across Europe. Absent far north.
FOOD/HABITS Queens visit sallow
catkins in March and April; workers
visit apple and cherry blossom.
Nests well below ground level.

Field bumble bee
Bombus pascuorum
SIZE AND DESCRIPTION Up to 18 mm long. Can be identified by its reddish-brown thorax (darker in the northern part of its range). Thin covering of brownish hairs on abdomen.
HABITAT Well-vegetated habitats, but not in exposed places.
FOOD/HABITS Queens appear late March or April. Colonies live longer into autumn than other species. Nests in old birds' nests, nestboxes and long grasses at ground level.

Meadow bumble bee
Bombus pratorum
SIZE AND DESCRIPTION 16–18 mm long. Collar and second abdominal segment are yellow. Tip of the abdomen is orange brown.
HABITAT Well-vegetated habitats across Europe, but not Scotland and northern Scandinavia.
FOOD/HABITS Appears in early spring, establishing colonies in April and May. Very agile, it visits both long, tubular flowers and open flowers. Nests on, below or above ground, including nestboxes.

Garden bumble bee
Bombus hortorum
Size and description 20–24 mm long. Collar, rear of thorax and first segment of abdomen are yellow. The tip of the abdomen is whitish. Scruffy appearance.
Habitat Common in well-vegetated habitats, especially in gardens, throughout Europe.
Food/habits Queens often seen on white dead-nettle. Nests on or just beneath the ground.

Leaf-cutter bee
Megachile centuncularis
SIZE AND DESCRIPTION 10–12 mm long.
Dark coloured above, but the female
has an orange pollen brush under the
abdomen.
HABITAT Woods, gardens and parks
across Europe.
FOOD/HABITS Flies May to August,
visiting a range of flowers. Female uses
its jaws to cut elliptical or round
sections from the leaves and petals of
roses and other plants. The leaf pieces
are then used to make sausage-shaped
cells for the bee grubs.

Cuckoo bee
*Psithyrus
barbutellus*
SIZE AND
DESCRIPTION
20 mm long.
Resembles *Bombus
hortorum* (see opposite),
but is less hairy. The black
abdomen has a white tip.
HABITAT Gardens, parks and open
country across Europe.
FOOD/HABITS Parasitises *Bombus
hortorum* by laying eggs in the
nest, often killing the queen. The bumble bee
workers then rear the cuckoo bee's grubs as if
they had been laid by the original queen.

Honey bee
Apis mellifera

Size and description 12–15 mm long. Queens are about 20 mm long, but are rarely seen outside the nest. Colours vary from dark brown to orange. Can be identified by the narrow cell near the tip of the wing's leading edge. Males have stouter bodies than females.

Habitat A native of south-eastern Europe, the honey bee is now found almost everywhere.

Food/habits Flies spring to late autumn. Lives in colonies with a single queen. Males, or drones, appear in spring and summer in small numbers. Nests contain combs of hexagonal cells, which are used for rearing grubs and storing pollen and honey.

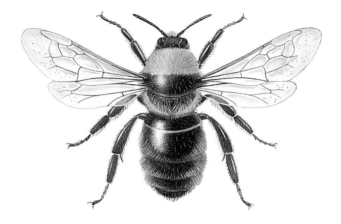

Cuckoo bee

Psithyrus campestris

SIZE AND DESCRIPTION 15–17 mm long. The thorax has yellowish hairs behind the head and grey hairs in front of the abdomen, which is largely shiny and hairless. The male is smaller than the female and varies in colour from yellow to black. Does not look like its host bumble bee.

HABITAT Most habitats, but avoids exposed places. Throughout Europe, but not Scotland and northern Scandinavia.

FOOD/HABITS Parasitises *Bombus pascuorum*.

Furniture beetle
Anobium punctatum
SIZE AND DESCRIPTION 2.5–5 mm long.
Colour of elytra varies from dark
brown to yellowish. Elytra are ridged.
Antennae are clubbed. Covered with
fine down.
HABITAT Dry wood of deciduous and
coniferous trees. Abundant in houses.
Central and northern Europe.
FOOD/HABITS Seen May to July. Larvae
are woodworm. Their presence is
shown only by the escape holes of
the emerging adults, which are
1.5–2 mm in diameter.

Larder beetle
Dermestes lardarius
SIZE AND DESCRIPTION 7–9.5 mm long.
The larder is an oval-shaped beetle.
The pale markings on the elytra may
be greenish, greyish or brownish.
Larvae is short and covered in hairs.
HABITAT Found in houses and also birds'
nests. Central and northern Europe.
FOOD/HABITS Found all year round,
with both larvae and adults feeding on
carrion and dried meats in store.
In houses, the larvae feed on
animal products.

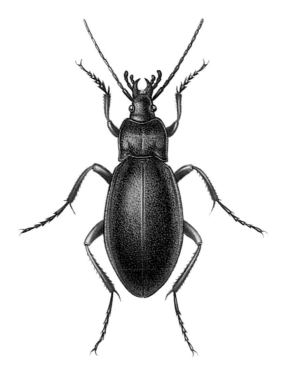

Violet ground beetle
Carabus violaceus
SIZE AND DESCRIPTION 20–35 mm long. Black all over, with violet tinges to the thorax and elytra. The thorax is flanged and the elytra has a smooth oval shape. Larva has a shiny black head and thorax, and a long, dusky, segmented body.
HABITAT Woods, hedges, gardens and scrub.
FOOD/HABITS Non-flying, fast-running, nocturnal predator of invertebrates. Larva is also a predator, but is less agile.

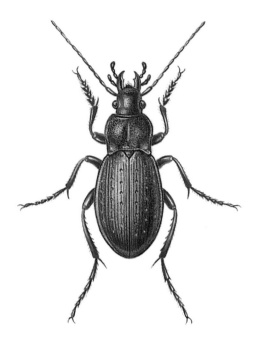

Carabid beetle
Carabus nemoralis

SIZE AND DESCRIPTION 20–30 mm long. Black, tinged with metallic colours varying from bronze to brassy green. Elytra are pitted in lines and finely ridged. Females are less shiny than males.

HABITAT Most habitats across Europe, except northern Scandinavia.

FOOD/HABITS The carabid is a fast-moving, flightless beetle. It is a nocturnal predator of ground-living invertebrates.

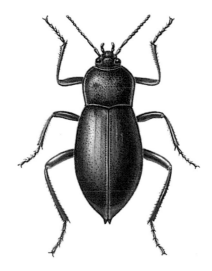

Churchyard beetle

Blaps mucronata

SIZE AND DESCRIPTION 18 mm long. Entirely black, with pitted elytra that taper at the ends to form a pointed tip.

HABITAT Dark places such as caves, cellars and stables in northern and central Europe.

FOOD/HABITS A nocturnal, flightless scavenger on vegetable matter. Emits a foul smell when threatened.

Devil's coach horse

Staphylinus olens

SIZE AND DESCRIPTION 20–30 mm long. Black, with small, almost square elytra, which leave the long abdomen exposed.

HABITAT Woods, hedges, parks and gardens across Europe. Often found in damp outhouses.

FOOD/HABITS Nocturnal predator with powerful jaws. Feeds on slugs and other invertebrates. When under threat, the beetle raises its tail and opens its jaws.

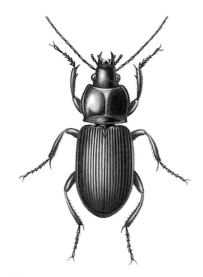

Black beetle
Feronia nigrita
SIZE AND DESCRIPTION
16 mm long. Jet black, with ridges
running down the elytra.
HABITAT Woods, gardens, and parks
across Europe.
FOOD/HABITS Nocturnal predator
of other invertebrates.

Oxytelus laquaetus
SIZE AND DESCRIPTION 6 mm long. A
rove beetle with small brown elytra
and yellowish legs.
HABITAT Compost heaps in gardens.
FOOD/HABITS Feeds on rotting
vegetable material and the grubs
of other insects in manure heaps.
Flies well.

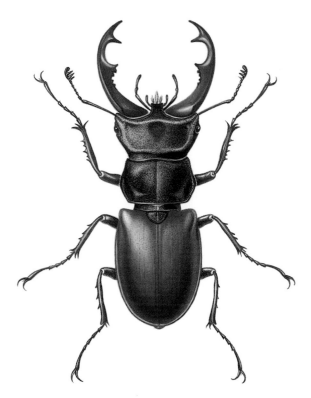

Stag beetle
Lucanus cervinus

SIZE AND DESCRIPTION 25–75 mm long. Smooth, dark-tan elytra, black head and thorax. Male's huge jaws look like antlers (hence the name). Whitish larva has a brown head.
HABITAT Oakwoods, parks and gardens. England, central and southern Europe. Becoming rare.
FOOD/HABITS Flies May to August, evenings and at night. Feeds on tree sap. Breeding males battle with "antlers". Larvae eat rotting wood.

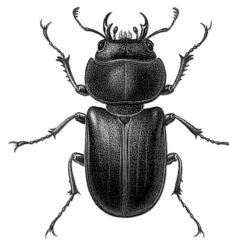

Lesser stag beetle
Dorcas parallelipipedus
SIZE AND DESCRIPTION 19–32 mm long.
Black and similar to the female stag
beetle, but has only one spur on the
tibia of its middle legs. Males have a
particularly wide head.
HABITAT Deciduous woods, parks
and gardens in northern and
central Europe.
FOOD/HABITS Flies April to October.
Feeds on sap. Larvae live in
rotting wood.

Rose chafer
Cetonia aurata
SIZE AND DESCRIPTION 14–18 mm long.
The flattened, squarish elytra are green,
but may be bronze or bluish-black.
HABITAT Woodland margins, hedges,
scrub and gardens in southern and
central Europe, including southern
England.
FOOD/HABITS Adults fly May to August
by day and nibble the petals and
stamens of flowers. Larvae feed in
decaying wood.

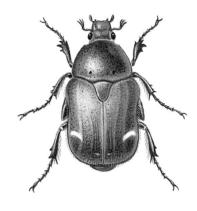

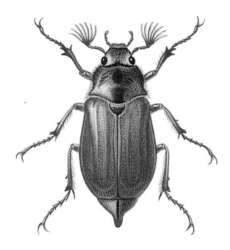

Cockchafer
Melolontha melolontha

SIZE AND DESCRIPTION 20–30 mm long. Black thorax. The rusty elytra do not quite cover the abdomen, exposing the pointed tip. Its legs are brown and the antennae fan out. Males have larger antennae than females. The whitish larva has a brown head, but is smaller and more wrinkly than the stag beetle larva.

HABITAT Woodland margins, parks and gardens. Common throughout Europe, but absent above 1,000 m and from northern Scandinavia.

FOOD/HABITS Also called the Maybug. Flies May to July at night. Adults chew leaves of trees and shrubs. Larvae, which take three years to develop, feed on roots.

Click beetle
Athous haemorrhoidalis
SIZE AND DESCRIPTION 7–10 mm long. A
long, black or dark brown thorax and a
brown, ridged back. Larva is brown,
with a thin, segmented body.
HABITAT Grassland, including parks and
gardens, across Europe, except for
northern Scandinavia.
FOOD/HABITS Flies May to July. Adults
chew grasses and flowers, especially
stamens with pollen. Larvae cause
severe damage to roots. Click beetles
are so-called because they can flip
themselves into the air when under
attack or threat.

Agriotes lineatus
SIZE AND DESCRIPTION 7.5–10 mm long.
Bullet-shaped, with lined elytra. Thorax
is black or brown.
HABITAT Grassland and cultivated land
in central and northern Europe.
FOOD/HABITS Seen throughout most of
the year, but is commonest from May
to August. The larvae, commonly
known as "wireworms", can be a
serious pest to cultivated plants.

Cardinal beetle
Pyrochroa coccinea
SIZE AND DESCRIPTION 14–18 mm long. Bright reddish-orange elytra and thorax, with a black head and feathery antennae. Black legs. Larvae are yellowish brown with squarish rear ends.
HABITAT Woodland edges in central and northern Europe.
FOOD/HABITS Flies May to July. Found on flowers and old tree-trunks. Larvae live under bark and prey on other insects.

Soldier beetle
Cantharis rustica
SIZE AND DESCRIPTION 11–14 mm long. Black elytra. The orange thorax bears a dark mark. Beaded antennae. Larva has flattened, segmented dark brown body with a pair of legs on each of the first three segments.
HABITAT Abundant throughout Europe in damp situations, including woodland edges and open country.
FOOD/HABITS Flies May to August. Preys on other insects, found on flower blooms.

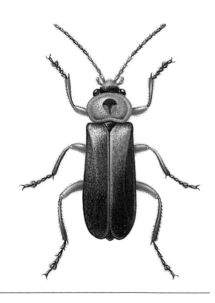

Two-spot ladybird
Adalia bipunctata
SIZE AND DESCRIPTION 3.5–5.5 mm long.
Varies greatly, with northern
populations often being largely black.
The most common form is red with a
bold black spot on each elytron. Larva
is similar to the seven-spot ladybird's.
HABITAT Well-vegetated habitats across
Europe. Abundant.
FOOD/HABITS Flies spring to autumn,
eating aphids on herbaceous and
woody plants. Winters in groups
(sometimes containing as many as
a thousand individuals) in sheds
and houses. Sites are used by
successive generations.

Seven-spot ladybird
Coccinella 7-punctata
SIZE AND DESCRIPTION
5.2–8 mm long. Bright-red elytra, with
seven black spots. Larva is steely blue,
with yellow or cream spots.
HABITAT Well-vegetated habitats
throughout Europe. Abundant.
FOOD/HABITS Flies early spring to
autumn. Both adults and larvae feed on
aphids. Winter is passed in small groups
or individually in leaf litter and
sheltered places near to the ground.

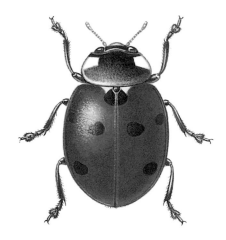

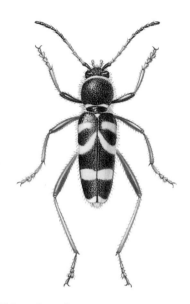

Wasp beetle
Clytus arictis
SIZE AND DESCRIPTION 7–14 mm long.
Black, with very variable yellow bands
on its elytra. Long-legged.
HABITAT Woods, gardens, parks and
hedges across Europe, except northern
Scandinavia.
FOOD/HABITS Seen May to July, often
feeding on flower nectar and pollen.
Female lays eggs in dead wood. A
harmless wasp-mimic.

Potato flea beetle
Psylliodes affinis
SIZE AND DESCRIPTION 2.8 mm long. A
reddish-brown beetle, with thick black
thighs on its hind legs.
HABITAT Common on nightshades and
potatoes in continental Europe.
FOOD/HABITS Adults nibble leaves, while
larvae feed on roots. Beetles hibernate
under bark and leaf litter, emerging in
spring to resume feeding.

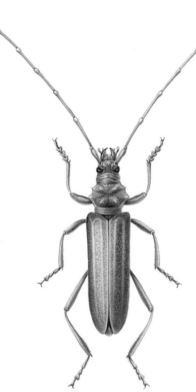

Musk beetle
Aromia moschata

SIZE AND DESCRIPTION 13–34 mm long. Striking metallic green or blue. Antennae as long as, or longer than, the combined head and body length.

HABITAT Deciduous woodland especially willow, across central Europe. Local in southern Britain.

FOOD/HABITS Flies June to August. Emits a musky secretion. The larvae develop in willows, particularly old pollards.

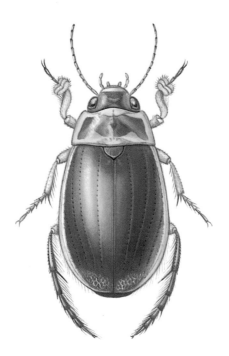

Great diving beetle
Dytiscus marginalis
SIZE AND DESCRIPTION 27–35 mm long. Very dark brown to black, fringed with yellowish-brown. Females have ridged elytra and males smooth. Larva has well-developed legs and a segmented body that bends more than that of a dragonfly nymph.
HABITAT The commonest European diving beetle. Prefers reedy ponds and other still waters.
FOOD/HABITS Flies at night. Preys on newts, tadpoles, fish and invertebrates. Larvae live underwater and are voracious predators.

Pea weevil
Sitona lineatus
SIZE AND DESCRIPTION 4–5 mm long. Pale and dark brown stripes run along the body. The eyes are very prominent.
HABITAT Found wherever wild and cultivated leguminous plants grow. Absent from northern Scandinavia.
FOOD/HABITS Adults, which are mainly active in spring and autumn, chew semi-circular pieces from the edges of leaves and may damage seedlings. The larvae live inside root nodules. There are several species of weevil that attack garden plants.

Nut weevil
Curculio nucum
SIZE AND DESCRIPTION 6–9 mm in length, including the "snout". The snout, or rostrum, is longer in females than in males. Feathery antennae stem from the rostrum.
HABITAT Woods, parks and gardens with oak and hazel. Central and northern Europe.
FOOD/HABITS Adults seen April to July visiting hawthorn blossom for nectar. The female uses her long snout to drill into a young hazel nut, and then lays an egg in the hole. The emerging larva feeds on the kernel until autumn, when the nut falls to the ground. The larva gnaws its way out of the nut and digs into the soil to pupate over winter.

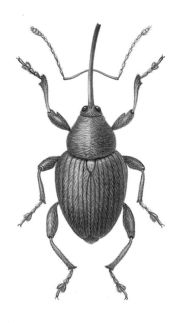

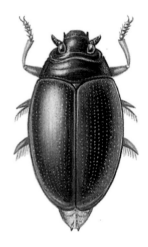

Whirligig beetle
Gyrinus natator
SIZE AND DESCRIPTION   6–7 mm long.
Tiny, shiny black beetle that gyrates on
the water's surface. Middle and hind
legs are short and oar-like. Two-part
eyes enable it to look down into the
water and across the surface
simultaneously.
HABITAT   Still and slow-moving water.
There are several European species.
FOOD/HABITS   Visible for much of the
year, but hibernates. Preys on mosquito
larvae and insects that fall into the
water. Often seen in small groups.
Dives if alarmed.

Hydroporus palustris
SIZE AND DESCRIPTION   3–3.3 mm long.
Oval-shaped elytra. Black, with patches
of orange or yellowish-brown. One of
34 species in a genus found in Europe.
HABITAT   Common in all types of still
water throughout Europe.
FOOD/HABITS   Preys on a variety of
small aquatic invertebrates. Flies at
night. Comes to the surface for air,
which it carries beneath its elytra in
a bubble when it dives.

Hydrobius fuscipes
SIZE AND DESCRIPTION 6 mm long. Black, with a metallic
sheen. Can be distinguished by the pitted furrows along the
elytra. The legs are rust coloured. The larva is maggot-like.
HABITAT Still waters across Europe.
FOOD/HABITS Omnivorous scavenger that does not swim
well and crawls over underwater plants. Collects air from
the surface by swimming to the surface head-first and
storing air beneath its elytra. Larvae are carnivores.

Addresses

Alana Ecology Ltd
The Old Primary School
Church Street
Bishop's Castle
Shropshire SY9 5AE
Tel 01588 630173
E-mail info@alanaecology.com
Website www.alanaecology.com

British Butterfly Conservation Society
Manor Yard
East Lulworth
Wareham
Dorset BH20 5QP
Tel 01929 400209
E-mail info@butterfly-conservation.org
Website www.butterfly-conservation.org

British Dragonfly Society
Secretary: Dr W H Wain
The Haywain
Hollywater Road
Bordon
Hampshire GU35 0AD
E-mail thewains@ukonline.co.uk
Website www.dragonflysoc.org.uk

Brunel Microscopes (BR) Ltd
Unit 6
Enterprise Centre
Chippenham
Wiltshire SN14 6QA
Tel 01249 462655
Fax 01249 445156
E-mail brunelmicro@compuserve.com
Website www.brunelmicroscopes.co.uk

The Microscope Shop
Oxford Road
Sutton, Scotney
Winchester
Hampshire SO21 3JG

NHBS
2-3 Wills Road
Totnes
Devon TQ9 5XN
Tel 01803 865913
E-mail nhbs@nhbs.co.uk
Website www.nhbs.com

Watkins & Doncaster
PO Box 5
Cranbrook
Kent TN18 5EZ
Tel 01580 753133
Fax 01580 754054
E-mail robin.ford@virgin.net
Website www.watdon.com
(General naturalists' supplies)

The Wildlife Trusts
The Kiln, Waterside
Mather Road
Newark
Nottinghamshire NG24 1WT
Tel 0870 036 7711
Fax 0870 036 0101
E-mail info@wildlife-trusts.cix.co.uk
Website www.wildlifetrusts.org

Wildlife Watch
(Contact details as above)
E-mail watch@wildlife-trusts.cix.co.uk

Suggested reading

Carter, D. & Hargreaves, B.
*A Field Guide to the Caterpillars of Butterflies
and Moths in Britain and Europe*
Collins, 1986

Chinery, Michael
Butterflies of Britain and Europe
Collins and The Wildlife Trusts, 1998

Chinery, Michael
*New Generation Guide to Butterflies and
Day-flying Moths of Britain and Europe*
Collins, 1989

Chinery, Michael
*Collins Guide to the Insects of Britain and
Western Europe*
Collins, 1986

Gilbert, Francis S.
Hoverflies
Richmond Publishing, 1993

Harde, K. W.
Beetles
Blitz Editions, 1999

Oxford, R.
*Minibeast Magic – Kind Hearted Capture
Techniques for Invertebrates*
Yorkshire Wildlife Trust, 1999

Packham, Chris
Chris Packham's Back Garden Nature Reserve
New Holland & The Wildlife Trusts, 2001

Powell, Dan
A Guide to the Dragonflies of Great Britain
Arlequin, 1999

Prys-Jones, Oliver E. & Corbet, Sarah A.
Bumblebees
Richmond Publishing, 1991

Redfern, Margaret & Askew, R. R.
Plant Galls
Richmond Publishing, 1998

Skinner, B.
*Colour Identification Guide to Moths
of the British Isles*
Viking, 1984

Wheater, C. P. & Read, H. J.
Animals under Logs and Stones
Richmond Publishing & The Company
of Biologists, 1996

Index